S. Emir Turna

Turkish Word Clauses For Part Of Speech Tagging

S. Emir Turna

Turkish Word Clauses For Part Of Speech Tagging

Easy to understand now

LAP LAMBERT Academic Publishing

Impressum / Imprint

Bibliografische Information der Deutschen Nationalbibliothek: Die Deutsche Nationalbibliothek verzeichnet diese Publikation in der Deutschen Nationalbibliografie; detaillierte bibliografische Daten sind im Internet über http://dnb.d-nb.de abrufbar.
Alle in diesem Buch genannten Marken und Produktnamen unterliegen warenzeichen-, marken- oder patentrechtlichem Schutz bzw. sind Warenzeichen oder eingetragene Warenzeichen der jeweiligen Inhaber. Die Wiedergabe von Marken, Produktnamen, Gebrauchsnamen, Handelsnamen, Warenbezeichnungen u.s.w. in diesem Werk berechtigt auch ohne besondere Kennzeichnung nicht zu der Annahme, dass solche Namen im Sinne der Warenzeichen- und Markenschutzgesetzgebung als frei zu betrachten wären und daher von jedermann benutzt werden dürften.

Bibliographic information published by the Deutsche Nationalbibliothek: The Deutsche Nationalbibliothek lists this publication in the Deutsche Nationalbibliografie; detailed bibliographic data are available in the Internet at http://dnb.d-nb.de.
Any brand names and product names mentioned in this book are subject to trademark, brand or patent protection and are trademarks or registered trademarks of their respective holders. The use of brand names, product names, common names, trade names, product descriptions etc. even without a particular marking in this work is in no way to be construed to mean that such names may be regarded as unrestricted in respect of trademark and brand protection legislation and could thus be used by anyone.

Coverbild / Cover image: www.ingimage.com

Verlag / Publisher:
LAP LAMBERT Academic Publishing
ist ein Imprint der / is a trademark of
OmniScriptum GmbH & Co. KG
Heinrich-Böcking-Str. 6-8, 66121 Saarbrücken, Deutschland / Germany
Email: info@lap-publishing.com

Herstellung: siehe letzte Seite /
Printed at: see last page
ISBN: 978-3-659-78465-1

DETERMINATION OF TURKISH WORD CLAUSES FOR PART OF SPEECH TAGGING

by

S. Emir TURNA

July, 2011

İZMİR

DETERMINATION OF TURKISH WORD CLAUSES FOR PART OF SPEECH TAGGING

ABSTRACT

According to their types of duties in a sentence, the meaning of the sentence varies. Therefore, in order to determine the exact meaning of the words in a sentence, the type and duty of the words should be examined. After the type determination process, the word phrases can be obtained.

In Turkish, depending on the word combinations, different word phrases can be occurred based on the types of the words. For this reason, all phrase possibilities should be considered during type determination process. After determining the word phrases, word clauses can be detected.

The most common problem faced in Natural Language Processing studies for Turkish is ambiguity problem. By determining word clauses, the ambiguities can be mainly solved and most exact meanings of the words can be determined.

In this study, rule based algorithm for determinant of word clauses in Turkish and software based on this algorithm was developed. It was seen that, by adding more rules to the system, the results are getting more reliable.

Key words: Natural Language Processing; Part Of Speech Tagging; Word Phrase

CONTENTS

CHAPTER ONE

INTRODUCTION

People always communicate with each other no matter which language it is. Natural Language Processing can help people for the purpose of communication. People speaking different languages can understand each other with NLP easily. For this purpose, NLP explains communication types and rules for people. In recent years, computer technology entered into a new path to ease the connection between people. Since people have different languages and different speech features, NLP and NLP studies are needed.

NLP has different research areas. Phonological studies, suffix-root structure, morphological structure, phrase structure and syntax, text summarization, word accent are some of these areas. These areas have different meaning for every language, because of these languages' structure differences. In shortly NLP examines languages and gives some solutions in many areas for people communication and understanding each other.

In this study, finding word phrases has priority. There are various NLP studies related to phrases and phrase structure studies are of great significance in sentence parsing. A phrase can change meaning of sentence or help understand what the sentence is about. So every possibility for phrase structure sould be found within a sentence and then these possibilities can help to explore the sentence as a whole.

This study aims at developing an algorithm to generate the ideal way in finding phrases in a sentence. The method developed here uses N-Gram analyze and root-suffix algorithm for the most proper result. It takes a sentence as input and returns all possible phrases for this sentence; and the user can do n-gram research on these phrases.

This thesis is divided into 7 chapters. In Chapter 1, the thesis statement is and the main purpose of the study is introduced and explained in brief. In Chapter 2, the related literature is reviewed. This chapter includes different approaches and their examples. In chapter 3, the possible application areas of phrase structure is discussed. Some determinations and some rules about phrase structure are given in chapter 4. Word phrase's meaning and N-Gram analyses are also provided in this chapter. In chapter 5 project's algorithms and the path for obtaining the results are presented. Chapter 6 comprises of application examples. Finally, last chapter presents the conclusions.

CHAPTER TWO

RELATED WORK

2.1 Illinois University Part Of Speech Tagger

In this application, which is developed in Illinois University, all words are analyzed in a text and their categories are returned to user. The application searches whole text for the words, which are defined and named 'key', and shows user another text. This text includes words which are represented with these keys. This study is about single words instead of word groups; and it works for English only (Rizzolo & Roth 2010). Keys of this study can be seen in table 2.1.

Input: Hello World

Output: UH Hello NNP World

Table 2.1 Key Words

Sign	Meaning	Sign	Meaning
"	Close Double Quote	``	Open double quote
'	Close single quote	`	Open single quote
,	Comma	.	Final punctuation
:	Colon, semi-colon	LRB	Left bracket
RRB	Right bracket	CC	Coordinating conjunction
CD	Cardinal number	DT	Determiner
EX	Existential there	FW	Foreign word
IN	Preposition	JJ	Adjective
JJR	Comparative adjective	JJS	Superlative adjective
LS	List Item Marker	MD	Modal
NN	Singular noun	NNS	Plural noun
NNP	Proper singular noun	NNPS	Proper plural noun
PDT	Predeterminer	POS	Possesive ending
PRP	Personal pronoun	PP$	Possesive pronoun
RB	Adverb	RBR	Comparative adverb
RBS	Superlative Adverb	RP	Particle
SYM	Symbol	TO	To
UH	Interjection	VB	Verb, base form
VBD	Verb, past tense	VBG	Verb, gerund /present participle
VBN	Verb, past participle	VBP	Verb, non 3rd ps. sing. Present
VBZ	Verb, 3rd ps. sing. Present	WDT	wh-determiner
WP	wh-pronoun	WP$	Possesive wh-pronoun
WRB	wh-adverb		

2.2 Part Of Speech Tagger and Chunker for Tamil Language

This study is done in India for Tamil language. It is ruuned with 60.000 words. It returns a text in which words are tagged according to their categories (Dhanalakshmi & Anand Kumar & Rejendran & Soman, 2009).

2.3 Stanford Log-Linear Part-Of-Speech Tagger

This application examines the words in the text, and assigns them different parts-of-speech to each word such as noun, verb and adjective. Since year 2004, seven different versions of this application were developed. The last known version was announced on 21.05.2010 at Stanford University. This application uses Penn Treebank set. (Stanford 2010). Penn Treebank tags are in the table 2.2.

Table 2.2 Penn Treebank Tags

Tag	Meaning	Tag	Meaning
CC	Coordinating conjunction	PRP$	Possessive pronoun
CD	Cardinal number	RB	Adverb
DT	Determiner	RBR	Adverb, comparative
EX	Existential	RBS	Adverb, superlative
FW	Foreign word	RP	Particle
IN	Preposition	SYM	Symbol
JJ	Adjective	TO	*To*
JJR	Adjective, comparative	UH	Interjection
JJS	Adjective, superlative	VB	Verb, base form
LS	List item marker	VBD	Verb, past tense
MD	Modal	VBG	Verb, gerund or present part.
NN	Noun, singular or mass	VBN	Verb, past participle
NNS	Noun, plural	VBP	Verb, non-3rd person sing. Pre

NNP	Proper noun, singular	VBZ	Verb, 3rd person sing. pre.
NNPS	Proper noun, plural	WDT	Wh-determiner
PDT	Predeterminer	WP	Wh-pronoun
POS	Possessive ending	WP$	Possessive wh-pronoun
PRP	Personal pronoun	WRB	Wh-adverb

Input: *A passenger plane has crashed shortly after take-off from Kyrgyzstan's Capital, Bishkek, killing a large number of those on board. The head of Kyrgyzstan's civil aviation authority said that out of about 90Passengers and crew, only about 20 people have survived. The Itek Air Boeing 737 took off bound for Mashhad, in north-eastern Iran, but   turned Round   some 10 minutes later.*

Output: *A_DT passenger_NN plane_NN has_VBZ crashed_VBN shortly_RB after-off_IN take-off_NN from_IN Kyrgyzstan_NNP 's_POS capital_NN ,_ , Bishkek_NNP ,_ , killing_VBG a_DT large_JJ number_NN of_IN those_DT on_IN board_NN ._ .*

The_DT head_NN of_IN Kyrgyzstan_NNP 's_POS civil_JJ aviation_NN authority_NN said_VBD that_IN out_IN of_IN about_IN 90_CD passengers_NNS and_CC crew_NN ,_ , only_RB about_IN 20_CD people_NNS have_VBP survived_VBN ._ .

The_DT Itek_NNP Air_NNP Boeing_NNP 737_CD took_VBD off_RP bound_VBN for_IN Mashhad_NNP ,_ , in_IN north-eastern_JJ Iran_NNP ,_ , but_CC turned_VBD round_NN some_DT 10_CD minutes_NNS later_RB ._ .

2.4 CLAWS Part Of Speech Tagger for ENGLISH

This work is done on huge corpus. This corpus has been upgrading since 1980, and at the last upgrade, the number of words was 100 million. The error rate of finding exact result on all samples tested is between %1.5 and %3.3. It uses a tag set which has 132 different key words (Garside & Leech & Sampson, 1987).

Input: Hello World

Output: Hello_NP0 World_NN1

2.5 Part Of Speech Tagger for Turkish

This work was done at 2006 at Boğaziçi University. ODTÜ-Sabancı Treebank was used for research. Its success rate was 77% (Altınyurt & Orhan, 2006).

Input   : Yeni bir döneme kayıt zamanında ders ekleme bırakma süresinde veya..

Output : *yeni N N ADJ*

        bir N

        dOneme N V

        kayIst N V

        zamanInda N N

        ders N

        ekleme N V N

        bIrakma V N

        sUresinde N ADJ   veya CON

Algorithm of the application is shown in figure 2.1;

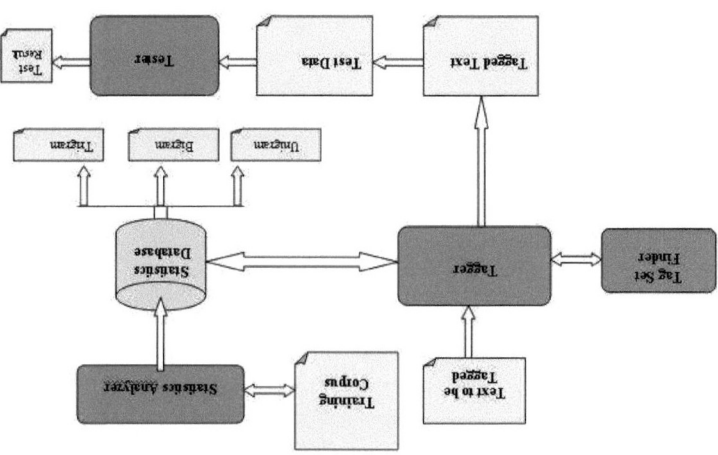

Figure 2.1

POS Tagger in Turkish algorithm

2.6 Hidden Markov Models

Hidden Markov Model was used in the mid-1980s in Europe. This model implements a statistical structure, and tries estimating categories of words according to their order in statement.

For example, it is calculated that article 'the' is followed by a noun for 40%, by an adjective for 40%, by a number for 20%. Then they could estimate the category of word which is after few words, not just after one word. CLAWS method is developed with inspiration by Hidden Markov Models. Many probability of words order can be calculated in a sentence (Charniak 1997, DeRose 1988).

2.7 Dynamic Programming Method

This algorithm was implemented at 1987 by Steven DeRose and Ken Church. In DeRose's control, word couples are used in table, and in Church's control, triple words are used in table. Their methods were succesful in many areas. In some rare circumtances, the model returns wrong results. These methods showed user that separating sentences in different degrees, is really important and useful (Charniak 1997, DeRose 1988).

2.8 Unsupervised Taggers

In this method, benefit of finding possibilities of previously used corpus is debated. This method argues that using unsupervised tagging, but tagging has to be changed according to using style. For example; 'a', 'an', 'the' morphemes are generally used in same meaning and function, statistically. But when they are used with other words, they can have very different meanings (Charniak 1997, DeRose 1988).

2.9 Trigram Taggers

Words are tagged statistically in this method. Next word is tried to guess according to current word. It can be thought as upgraded version Markov Model. This method is more successful than other algoriths whch are implemented for daily language (Brant, 2000).

2.10 Tree Tagger

This study is a successful example about tagging words and reaching header information. It is proved that this method is successful in many languages. German, English, French, Italian, Dutch, Spanish, Bulgarian, Russian, Greek, Portuguese, Chinese, Swahili, Latin, Estonian and old French are some of these languages. It can be adapted to other languages. In this study, categories are placed in a tree which is structured statistically (Schmid 1993). Example is shown in Figure 2.2

Exp:

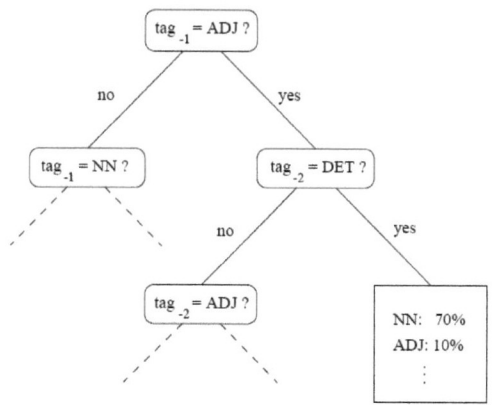

Figure 2.2 Tree Tagger algorithm

Output:

word	pos	lemma
word	*pos*	*lemma*
The	*DT*	*the*
TreeTagger	*NP*	*TreeTagger*
is	*VBZ*	*Be*
easy	*JJ*	*easy*
to	*TO*	*To*
use	*VB*	*Use*
.SENT.		

14

2.11 Comparison

In algorithms, which are explained above, it is understood that there are different structures which are used for tagging words. Some of the algorithms decide the categories of words by investigating words on their own. However, some of them examine more than one word; investigate their order in the sentences and their probability of following each other. Unfortunately all of the algorithms given above have some missing points.

If a word's category is checked from a corpus or a tag set, result for word phrases can't be returned rightly. Because of this, side by side two words can have completely different meaning according to these two words' own meanings.

While working with statistical information, results are never exactly correct, and the results can be wrong when they are used for daily language or when it is used with different word categories.

CHAPTER THREE

WORD PHRASES AND N-GRAM ANALYSIS

3.1 Word Phrase Determination

Word phrases are generated from words for developing the word's meaning. Word phrases create a hierarchical relationship between concepts. So they choose induction from the simple part.

Phrases in a sentence may serve different functions. Some of them specifiy other words and some indicate a words' judgment. Words with same or different functionality can generate phrases. Formation of word phrases is based on some rules of Turkish syntax. The basic rule of Turkish Syntax is the predicate, the main element of a sentence is at the end of the sentence. Word phrases are adjacent words that are together for specifying an attribute, a situation, a motion, a concept within certain rules (Yüzübenli, 2006).

Attributes, situations, motions and concepts can be specified via a word. But if that word is not enough to define them, then a word phrase may serve this function.

At this point, there are some important cases. These are;

a)   Word phrases behave like a word in a sentence and in other word phrases.

b)   Arrangement of words is regular within a group.

c)   The suffix at the end of the word phrase belongs to all words not the last one.

3.2 Types of Word Phrases

In Turkish syntax the main phrase structure is the head of the phrase is always at the right, so the complementary elements come before the head of the phrase. This situation changes only for compound sentences with 'ki' clitic. This order is also time order. According to this information there are different types of word phrases about meanings or mission in sentence (İbrahimoğlu 2008).

Possessive Noun Phrase;

It contains two words. First word's meaning is determined with adding a possessive suffix and completed with another noun. Because of first one has possessive, this is also called 'possessive subordinative'

Exp: Çoğu İnsan   Canım Kardeşim

        Most People   *Dear Brother*

        Kimi Gençler   Güzelim Çocuklar

        Some Young People   *Beautiful Children*

Specifier Phrase;

A noun with '-i' suffix, pronoun and adjective generate this phrase. It can be considered like an adjective phrase. In this phrase, the specifier is also a phrase.

Exp: Yazıyı Yazan 'Öğrenci'   Seni Soran 'Adam'

        Writing Student   *Asking you men*

Dative Phrase;

It is an adjective phrase with '-e' suffix. Dative noun, an adjective or inertial with an adjective mission create this phrase.

Exp: Yanına Yaklaşılmaz 'Fiyatlar'

        Unapproachable prices

Locative Phrase;

Noun with '-de' suffix and an adjective or participle generate this.

Exp: Sözde 'Aydınlar'   Yolda 'Yürüyenler'

        So-called intellectuals   *walkers on the road*

Ablative Phrase;

Its elements are noun with '-den' suffix and an adjective or participle.

Exp: Gözden Düşmüş 'İnsan'   Yoldan Çıkmış 'Biri'

Discredited human   *someone way out*

In this phrase there is a comparison between person mentioned in the sentence and the others. Whole words or some of them can be used like a subordinative and this phrase adds 'from between' meaning to that subordinatve.

Preposition Phrase;

A noun or a noun phrase and a preposition define this. These phrases behave like an adjective or an adverb. This phrase was used as 'İÖ' in this study.

Exp: Sana Göre İş   Ev İçin Kapı

Job for you   *door for home*

Conjunction Phrase;

This phrase has close, same, opposite meaning words in the same type. These words merge with a conjunction.

Exp: "Sevinç ve mutlulukların sonu"   "Kitap okunması ve eleştirilmesi"

end of joy and happiness   *reading and critique of book*

Adverb Phrase;

An adjective, a noun and an adverb are elements or this. This phrase is used as 'BÖ' in this study.

Exp: "Çok çalışkan 'öğrenci'"   "En güzel 'gün'"

very hardworking student   *most beautiful day*

Exclamation Phrase;

A noun or a noun phrase and an exclamation expression generate this phrase. Exclamation is just one word.

Exp: Ey, bu topraklar için toprağa düşmüş asker!

You, fallen soldier for this land!

Title (Honorific) Phrases;

Elements of these phrases are person names and their titles. Title word behaves like an adjective in the phrase. Titles can be before or after name.

Exp: Bayan Sevgi, Dr. Ali...   Begüm Sultan, Osman Gazi...

            Miss Sevgi, Dr. Ali   *Sultan Begüm, Ghazi Osman*

Intensifiers;

Intensifiers can be created with, first syllable plus 'p' letter for words starting with a vowel or the first syllable plus 'm,p,r,s' letters for words starting with a consonant.

Exp: Ak – apak   İri – ipiri   Uzun – upuzun

       white   *big*   *tall*

Adjective Phrase;

An adjective or an adverb plus an adjective can create an adjective phrase. This phrase is used as 'SÖ' in this study.

Exp   :   Mavi   Çok güzel

           Blue   *very nice*

Verb Phrase;

A verb alone or a verb with the other phrase can generate this phrase. This phrase is used as 'EÖ' in this study.

Exp: Geldi

       Came

Noun Phrase;

A combination of multiple nouns like genitive plus a noun or an adjective plus a noun can define the noun phrase. This phrase is used as 'AÖ' in this study.

Exp: Odanın Tavanı   Kapıcının Oğlu

ceiling of the room   *son of the doorman*

3.3 Word Order Rules

As mentioned before, order of the words in sentences depend on some syntactic rules.

It is called 'Regular Sentence' this kind of sentence.Word phrases can be found word phrases easily with these rules. These rules can be shown in table 3.1.

Table 3.1 General word order rules

T = AÖ + EÖ	
AÖ = A	Ali
AÖ = AÖ + A	Ali'nin arabası *Ali's car*
AÖ = SÖ + A	güzel kız *beautiful girl*
SÖ = S	Güzel *Nice*
SÖ = BÖ + S	çok güzel *very nice*
BÖ = B	çok,yavaş,ileri,az *many,slow,forward, less*
BÖ= BÖ + B	çok yavaş, daha hızlı *too slow, faster*

İÖ = AÖ + İ	araba ile (arabayla), okula doğru
	with car, through the school
EÖ= E	(Ali) düştü.
	(Ali) fell
EÖ= AÖ + E	(Ali) okula geldi.
	came to school
EÖ= AÖ + AÖ + E	(Ayşe) Ali'ye kazak ördü.
	(Ayşe) has knit a sweater for Ali
EÖ= AÖ + BÖ + E	(Ali) okula koşarak geldi.
	(Ali) came to school running
EÖ= AÖ + İÖ + E	(Ali) okula arabayla geldi.
	(Ali) came to school by car

As it can be seen in the first rule the table, a sentence is a noun phrase plus a verb phrase. This is because, canonical sentences in Turkish generally start with a noun phrase and end with a verb phrase, the verb or a copular noun being placed at the end. After finding this item, every word should be analyzed by itself and according to the word after it.

Every word can be a phrase by definiton. Therefore, when multiple words form a group, together they behave like one single word. So whole word phrase can be thought like one category of words.

The phrase structure is an iterative one; so if two words from the same category, they can create a new phrase in the category of the head word.

Exp: AÖ + A ☐ AÖ + A ☐ AÖ

When these word order rules are investigated, the word at the end determines the category of the phrase. So reverse order view brings the most accurate result when sentences or word are analyzed.

3.4 N-Gram Analysis and N-Gram in Phrases

3.4.1 What Is N-Gram?

One of the required data in many NLP studies like speech determination and machine translation is basic statistical information about the language. Simply, these systems need the probability of coincidence information of a word or words in a particular language. This information is obtained from a mechanism called Language Model. In this topic, a popular approach called 'N-Gram Language Model' is used widely due to its simplicity. Basically, this model reveals how often one, two or more words are found adjacent in a text (Güven & Bozkurt & Kalıpsız, 2006).

Exp: "kedi"   "Tekir kedi"   "Sevimli tekir kedi"

    Cat   *Tabby Cat*   *Cute Tabby Cat*

'N' means number of words in N-Gram word. In the examples above, "tekir kedi" is 2-grams or bigram, "sevimli tekir kedi" is 3-grams or "trigram".

This kind of statistics or information is generally obtained with counting number of adjacent words in large-scale texts. Naturally, probability of "tekir kedi" is greater than "tekir köpek" probability. "tekir" is an adjective which is generally used with "kedi".

N-Gram method is also used for determining the language of a text by a computer. Computers can do this with checking a word's letters' pattern.

Exp: Bilgisayar > 2 Gram > b bi il lg gi is sa ay ya ar r

> 3 Gram > b bil ilg lgi gis isa say aya yar r

Every language's words' N-Gram patterns like 2-Gram, 3-Gram are different. So with this approach a text's language can be discovered.

3.4.2 Importance of N-Gram in Phrases

If N-Gram method is used with phrases instead of a whole text, more meaningful and more logical results can be discovered compared to general outcomes.

After reaching significant word phrases according to adjacency rules, it will be very important to analyze these phrases via N-Gram method to examine the sentence or text, to summarize it, or understand the topic.

Exp: Dümenin terbiye edemediğini kayalar terbiye eder.

Those who will not be ruled by the rudder mist he ruled by the rock.

If N-Gram analyze is done to the whole sentence with whole words, some meaningless results will be got some meaningless results like 'dümenin terbiye' or 'kayalar terbiye'. But when same operation is done after finding word phrases, the results will change. This type of analysis is reached the more correct conclusions.

CHAPTER FOUR

STAGES OF WORD PHRASE DETERMINATION

4.1 Application Areas of Word Phrases

4.1.1 Sentence Meaning Analysis

If phrases of a sentence are found, meaning analysis will be easier. Since words have different meanings and different groupings, finding the sentence meaning is a difficult task. There are many options, so realizing what the most appropriate meaning of a word for the overall sentence meaning is takes too much time. Hovewer, if phrase structure of sentence is known, reaching the main point of sentence will be much simpler. Therefore word phrases lead to interpret the sentence semantically.

4.1.2 Word Accents

Phonologically every sentence can have nucleus, where the accent is placed on. This part of the sentence is the most prominent part. It is sometimes called the sentence accent. For many languages the sentence accent is fixed in position; however, under some certain circumstances this accent can move forth or backwards in the sentence. The knowledge of phrase structure enables to determine the position of the accent, sayingly on which word phrase the accent is.

In addition to sentence accent, words can have their own accent, too. In this situation phrase structure is of help again. If the phrase has more than one hierarchial layer, or has another phrase within it, phrase structure can show which word or phrase is more prominent or foregrounded.

4.1.3 Text Summarization Based On Semantic Analysis

When words or word groups are analyzed in a sentence using phrase structure, clues can be got about the text. Using word phrases and their meanings help to make meaningful and covering summarization. Consequently, summarization is a job to reveal a compressed text which represents a meaningful whole from the original text. Phrase structure is important in this task to define the most prominent words or word groups in the sentence that will be chosen for inclusion in the summary.

4.1.4 Finding Sentence Elements

When phrases are found, categories of words must be known. Due to these different categories, phrase categories vary too. If there is an adverb or a conjunction in a sentence, it is known that these words need complements to form a word group. In the same way, verbs make to think that there is a predicate and there are its complements. Via this method, the sentence can be separated into its sub-parts.

4.1.5 Text Classification

Different classification methods can be chosen according to the criteria in a text. These methods can change according to words' meaning in the text, their function in the text or even categories of words. These groupings can be used to get statistics or reach meaning of sentence. In this point, knowing phrases helps to understand word's meaning and category of the word. Instead of analyzing words alone, examining phrases can help to put the words to the right group according to determined classification method.

4.1.6 Access Right Meaning and Right Document (Information Retrieval)

Using phrases is very helpful to access words of sentence. Instead of whole words analysis, investigation of phrases gains time for reaching to the right place in the sentence or text.

4.2 Finding Phrases

The common tradition of word phrase naming is projecting the name of the head word category to the category of the phrase. In this case, firstly, categories of the words should be defined in a sentence and to find phrases these words form and than and at last classify these phrase. After identifying word categories, the phrase boundaries can be decided with adjecency rules according to these categories.

4.2.1 Rule Creation

When phrases are separated according their types, adjacency rules are not enough for judging; because, if words are adjacent just because of their types, meaningless word phrases may emerge. Therefore, for more specific and detailed results, general rules should be generated. The suffixed added to the adjacent words may give a clue about a general rule. Many rules should be developed like this. Rate of true return results can be increased with a rule-based system in new versions of project.

4.2.2 Effect of Punctuation Marks

In a sentence, comma between words functions as a separator. However, it is not always useful for exact and true solution.

Exp: Küçük okulu sevdi.   He/She liked small school

           Küçük, okulu sevdi.   *Little boy/girl liked school*

In these sentences, comma creates a different phrase structure. In the first sentence when there is no comma, 'küçük okul' is a noun phrase. But in the second one both of 'küçük' and 'okul' are noun phrases. On the other hand, in 'Ayşe güzel, alımlı ve bakımlı bir kızdır' ('Ayşe is a beautiful, charming and well-groomed girl'), sentence, comma does not change the structure but coordinates the adjectives. Because of these situations, when a sentence is examined, punctuation marks should be also evaluated.

4.3 Algorithms

4.3.1 Root-Suffix Algorithm

Sentence must be reviewed word by word for finding phrases. In this case, firstly, words of that sentence on the attempted. When phrases or subordinatives are defined, main criterion is the categories of words. So determining categories of words is the first task.

Categories or words can be changed according to these words' root, stem and suffixes. One suffix can change category or the stem of word can show its category due to its function.

The root and suffixes of each word to be analyzed isdetermined by a web service developed at Dokuz Eylül University Computer Engineering Department, which has known as "roots and suffixes"(Birant 2005), is used to examine root-to-stem transitions. This service takes a word as input and returns an XML code including that word's possible roots and possible suffixes. At the same time, some tags which are changeable according to suffix type are also provided with this data. It is very useful for finding suffix type and also the stem type.

Exp: Response from the Service for KIRMIZI Word (Birant 2005);

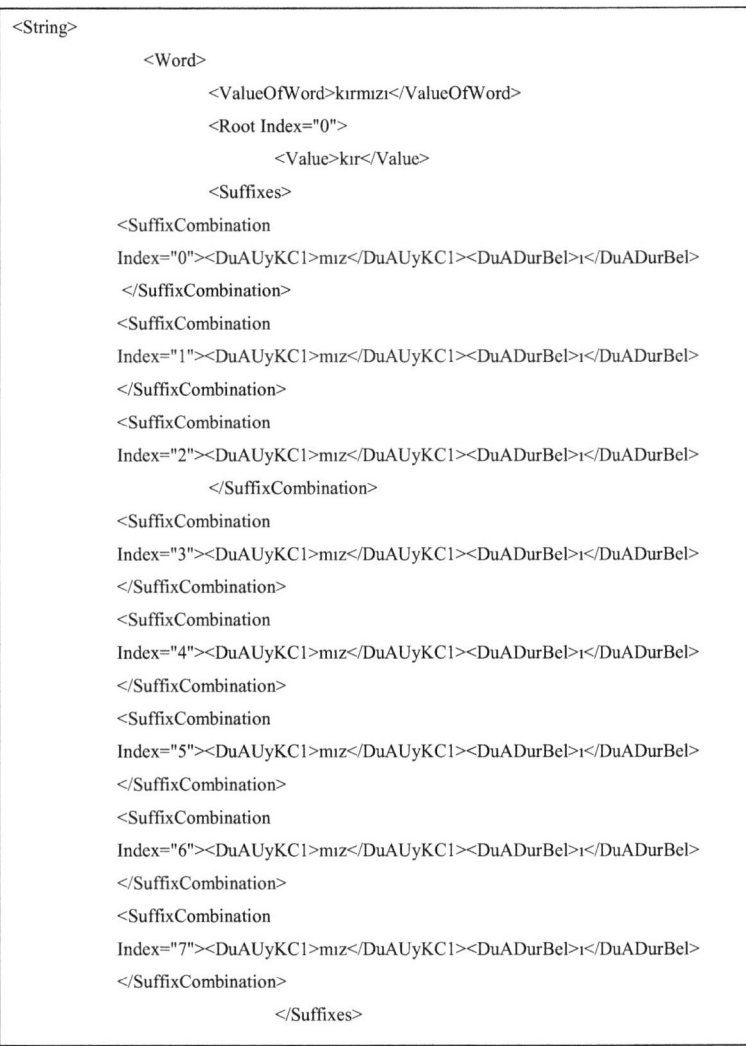

```
<String>
            <Word>
                  <ValueOfWord>kırmızı</ValueOfWord>
                  <Root Index="0">
                        <Value>kır</Value>
                  <Suffixes>
      <SuffixCombination
      Index="0"><DuAUyKC1>mız</DuAUyKC1><DuADurBel>ı</DuADurBel>
       </SuffixCombination>
      <SuffixCombination
      Index="1"><DuAUyKC1>mız</DuAUyKC1><DuADurBel>ı</DuADurBel>
      </SuffixCombination>
      <SuffixCombination
      Index="2"><DuAUyKC1>mız</DuAUyKC1><DuADurBel>ı</DuADurBel>
                  </SuffixCombination>
      <SuffixCombination
      Index="3"><DuAUyKC1>mız</DuAUyKC1><DuADurBel>ı</DuADurBel>
      </SuffixCombination>
      <SuffixCombination
      Index="4"><DuAUyKC1>mız</DuAUyKC1><DuADurBel>ı</DuADurBel>
      </SuffixCombination>
      <SuffixCombination
      Index="5"><DuAUyKC1>mız</DuAUyKC1><DuADurBel>ı</DuADurBel>
      </SuffixCombination>
      <SuffixCombination
      Index="6"><DuAUyKC1>mız</DuAUyKC1><DuADurBel>ı</DuADurBel>
      </SuffixCombination>
      <SuffixCombination
      Index="7"><DuAUyKC1>mız</DuAUyKC1><DuADurBel>ı</DuADurBel>
      </SuffixCombination>
                        </Suffixes>
```

Figure 4.1 The part of result file about the word "kırmızı"

```
                    </Root>
                    <Root Index="1">
                            <Value>kırmız</Value>
                            <Suffixes>
<SuffixCombination
Index="0"><DuAUyKC1>mız</DuAUyKC1><DuADurBel>ı</DuADurBel>
</SuffixCombination>
<SuffixCombination
Index="1"><DuAUyKC1>mız</DuAUyKC1><DuADurBel>ı</DuADurBel>
</SuffixCombination>
<SuffixCombination
Index="2"><DuAUyKC1>mız</DuAUyKC1><DuADurBel>ı</DuADurBel>
</SuffixCombination>
<SuffixCombination
Index="3"><DuAUyKC1>mız</DuAUyKC1><DuADurBel>ı</DuADurBel>
</SuffixCombination>
<SuffixCombination Index="4"><DuADurBel>ı</DuADurBel>
</SuffixCombination>
<SuffixCombination Index="5"><DuAUyKT3>ı</DuAUyKT3>
</SuffixCombination>
<SuffixCombination Index="6"><DuADurBel>ı</DuADurBel>
</SuffixCombination>
<SuffixCombination Index="7"><DuAUyKT3>ı</DuAUyKT3>
</SuffixCombination>
                            </Suffixes>
                    </Root>
            <Root Index="2">
                    <Value>kırmızı</Value>
                            <Suffixes>
<SuffixCombination
Index="0"><DuAUyKC1>mız</DuAUyKC1><DuADurBel>ı</DuADurBel>
</SuffixCombination>
<SuffixCombination
```

Figure 4.1 The part of result file about the word "kırmızı"

Index="1"><DuAUyKC1>mız</DuAUyKC1><DuADurBel>ı</DuADurBel>

</SuffixCombination>

<SuffixCombination

Index="2"><DuAUyKC1>mız</DuAUyKC1><DuADurBel>ı</DuADurBel>

</SuffixCombination>

<SuffixCombination

Index="3"><DuAUyKC1>mız</DuAUyKC1><DuADurBel>ı</DuADurBel>

</SuffixCombination>

<SuffixCombination Index="4"><DuADurBel>ı</DuADurBel>

</SuffixCombination>

<SuffixCombination Index="5"><DuAUyKT3>ı</DuAUyKT3>

</SuffixCombination>

<SuffixCombination Index="6"><DuADurBel>ı</DuADurBel>

</SuffixCombination>

<SuffixCombination Index="7"><DuAUyKT3>ı</DuAUyKT3>

</SuffixCombination>

</Suffixes>

</Root>

</Word>

</string>

Figure 4.1 The part of result file about the word "kırmızı"

As shown in the example, word's possible categories can be got from the response. Tags which are at the beginning of the suffix will bring the categories.

4.3.2 Obtaining Word Category Algorithm

Results from the root-suffix service should be separated for investigation. Firstly every root category and then all possible suffix combinations should be examined.

All of root possibilities is separated. After this operation, the word's formation is traced from root to stem step-by-step according to the categories of the suffixes and their function.

Suffix categories with their functions in sentences used in this study are taken from Birant (2005).

29

The type of suffix can be understood according to their first two letters of the tag. If two letters are 'DU' at the beginning, it is a grammatical category suffix; an inflectional suffix which does not change the category of word it is added. So root and root with suffix categories are the same after adding this kind of suffix. But if the first two letters in the tag are 'TB', it is understood that there is a new category of word since this suffix is a derivational suffix. Since last state of word is needed, after all suffixes; the final category of the word is the category after the last derivational suffix.

If these operations are done for all possible categories and for all root-suffix combinations, every kind of possible words will be had. As the final step, when this operation is applied for all words of the sentence, what kind of combinations there are in the sentence can be determined.

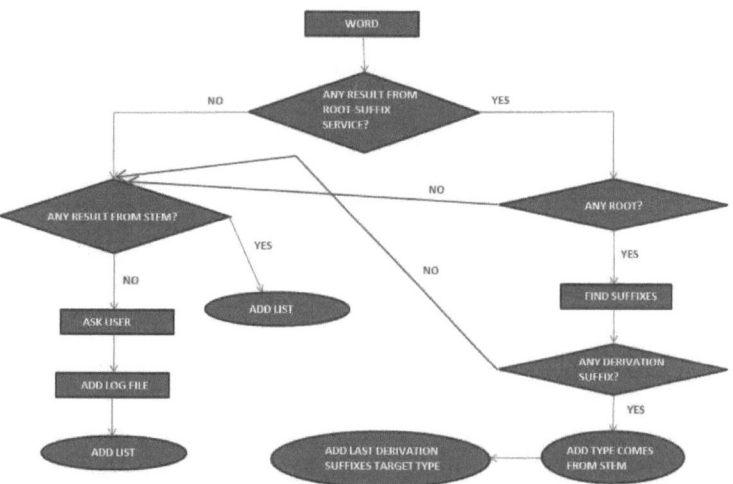

Figure 4.2 Obtaining Word Category Algorithm

4.3.3 Finding Categories From Word Stem

Word roots and suffixes are not enough to fully determine the category of the word, since some words may change category according to their function or their position in the sentence.

For instance, when 'Kırmızı'('red') Word is analyzed according its possible roots and suffixes, the result will be a noun but in some cases this word functions as an adjective. So just root and suffix analysis is not enough for determining a word's category. Different aspects are needed to check.

To solve this problem, another service, stems of each Word to be analyzed is determining by this service developed at Dokuz Eylül University Computer Engineering Department(Alkım 2011), can be used for returning stem type according to its function or position in the sentence or in a phrase. It serves other possible types.

Exp: KIRMIZI (RED)

Response From Service;

<string>isim(Noun)/sifat(Adjective)</string>

4.3.4 User Feedback

Another factor is user feedback. If suffixes are complicated, or the word is different than the words which are defined before, the answer may not return from service. Because of this inconclusive return is that service's corpus grows dynamically. If no result, this word and its solution are added to the service. In such situation, user feedback is waited for system continuity. The system asks the category of the word to the user and then goes on according to the reply. Additionally the system records the word into the system and then if same word is processed again, the system automatically assigns the category of the word.

4.3.5 Phrase Finding Algorithm

After determining the categories of words, word order can be examined and then these words can grouped according to phrase structure algorithms. It should be known that each word is a word phrase on its own. So if word is part of any word group before itself, it should be examined.

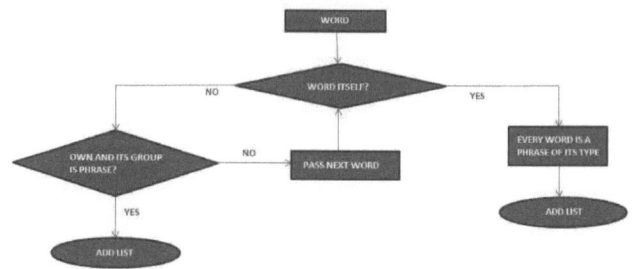

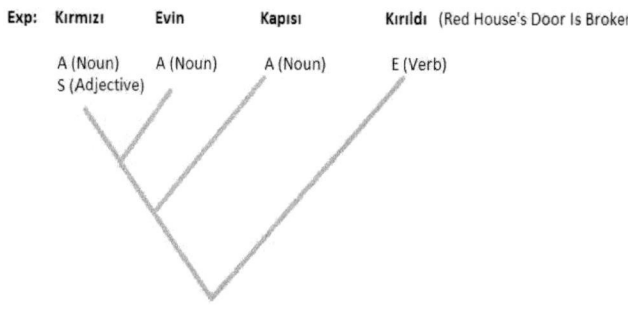

Figure 4.3 Phrase Finding Algorithm

CHAPTER FIVE

APPLICATION

In this study, one of Microsoft development tool was used. It is called Visual Studio .Net 2008. This tool has some programming languages for creating projects. C# is one of these languages and it is used in this study. Reason of this language usage is, C# is flexiable, popular and easy understanding.

A database is needed in this study to store some values and to reach them easily. MySQL database is used for this operation. This database system is harmonious with Microsoft tools and C# language. In addition to this feature, MySQL has quick search between table values.

5.1 Screen Shots

Splash Screen

When the application started, this screen will show on the screen firstly. The other pages can be reached from this page.

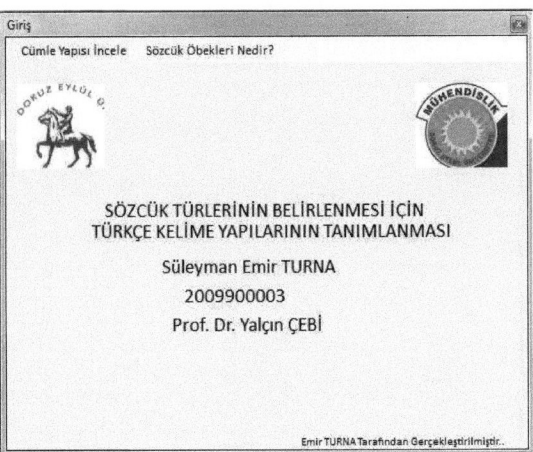

Figure 5.1 Splash Screen of the Project

Application Screen

That is the main screen for this application. The user writes the sentence and chooses which phrases user wants to see in that sentence.

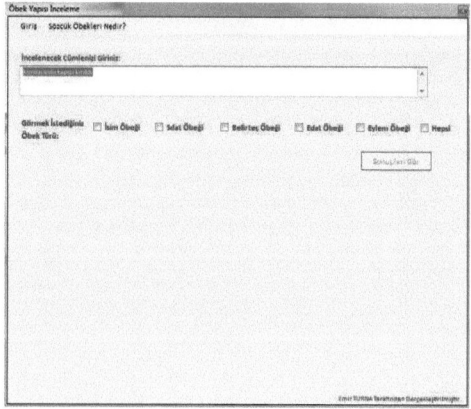

Figure 5.2 Application screen

User Support

If there is no result after root-suffix algorithm and stem search, the system asks the user to determine the category of the word.

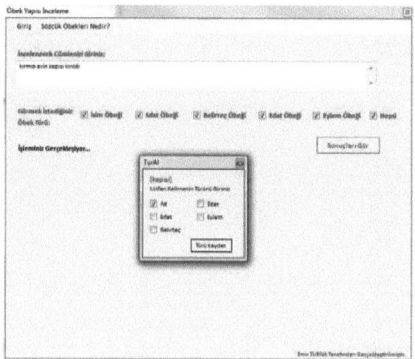

Figure 5.3 User support for undetermined categories

34

Category Probabilities

After the all possibility research, from root-suffix and stem types, the results will be presented on the screen for information to the user.

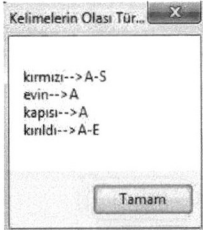

Figure 5.4 Category Prob.

Results Screen

After all operations on the sentence, some results are had according to rules. The categories of all the words and word phrases can be seen. Also, the statistical information can be controlled the statistical information about the N-Gram method.

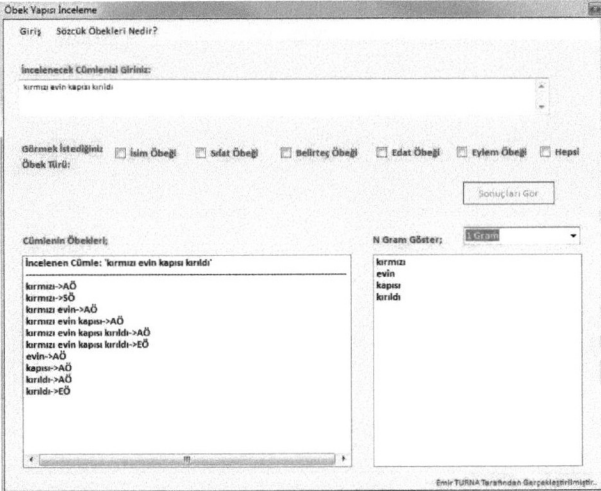

Figure 5.5 Result screen of the analyzed sentence

5.2 Application Samples

Sample 1

As seen in table 5.1, every word has their own word types. When sentence is examined for every type of words, many different results will be found. 'Kırıldı' (Broken) word is a verb and also a noun type in Turkish. Because of this, whole sentence can be noun phrase and also verb phrase. This is the reason of investigating all type probabilities.

Table 5.1 Sample 1

Sentence	"Kırmızı Evin Kapısı Kırıldı" *Red House's Door Is Broken*
Word Categories	"Kırmızı" → A-S *Red → Noun-Adjective* "Evin" → A *House → Noun* "Kapısı" → A *Door → Noun* "Kırıldı" → A-E *Broken → Noun-Verb*
Results	Kırmızı → AÖ *Red → Noun Phrase* Kırmızı → SÖ *Red → Adjective Phrase* Kırmızı Evin → AÖ *Red House → Noun Phrase*

36

	Kırmızı Evin Kapısı → AÖ
	Red House's Door → Noun Phrase
	Kırmızı Evin Kapısı Kırıldı → AÖ
	Red House's Door Is Broken → Noun Phrase
	Kırmızı Evin Kapısı Kırıldı → EÖ
	Red House's Door Is Broken → Verb Phrase
	Evin → AÖ
	House → Noun Phrase
	Kapısı →AÖ
	Door → Noun Phrase
	Kırıldı →AÖ
	Broken → Noun Phrase
	Kırıldı →EÖ
	Broken → Verb Phrase

Sample 2

Like at the first sample, last word of the sentence defines the sentence phrase category. This is a kind of regular sentence rule. In this study, regular sentences are used. So for every sample and sentence, searching of sentence can be started from the last word.

Table 5.2 Sample 2

Sentence	"Yeşil Işıkta Geçmek Gerekir"
	We must cross the street at the green light
Word Categories	"Yeşil" → S
	Green → Adjective
	"Işıkta" → A
	Light → Noun
	"Geçmek" → A
	Cross → Noun
	"Gerekir" → E
	Must → Verb
Result	Yeşil → SÖ
	Green → Adjective Phrase
	Yeşil Işıkta → AÖ
	Green Light → Noun Phrase
	Yeşil Işıkta Geçmek → AÖ
	Cross At The Green Ligh → Noun Phrase
	Yeşil Işıkta Geçmek Gerekir → EÖ
	Must Cross The Street At The Green Light → Verb Phrase
	Işıkta→ AÖ
	Light → Noun Phrase
	Geçmek→ AÖ

	Cross → *Noun Phrase*
	Gerekir → EÖ
	Must → *Verb Phrase*

Sample Comparison

As it can be seen from the examples given above, this study is usefull for regular sentences and known word categories. There is a result for every probability of word categories. If there is more than one category, sentence is examined for all categories.

There is an important detail about the word categorization in these examples. If there is a verb category before last word of the sentence, this category probability is not considered important, because of in regular sentences verb is at the end of the sentence.

CHAPTER SIX

CONCLUSION

In this study, a word phrase search tool was prepared to reach and understand a sentence meaning and structure. This tool needs a sentence as input and if necessary, user feedback, while processing a sentence operation. After this operation, words' categories of that sentence and word phrases of sentence are outputs.

Each word's meaning can change according to its root, suffixes, prefixes, and stems which are formed with these suffixes or prefixes, in Turkish. This new formed words can create word groups with different functions, according to its usage in sentences, its position in sentence, or the words accompanying it. So, firstly, the differences of word categories are needed to understand and the variety of word groups.

This study gives word phrases according to words' types by using simple word order rules. It gives a result with just one sentence as input. Its main duty is separating the sentences to words, than concatenating words according to their categories and presenting word phrases.

Finally, in order to specify the sentence rules, system efficiency and effectiveness should be increased. Moreover, after improving effectiveness, the system can help to develope other Natural Language Processing researchs like text summarization or information retrieval. In the future, after the improvements, this system may be used as a separated module or a part of a system.

REFERENCES

- Brants, T. (2000) TnT - A Statistical Part-of-Speech Tagger, Proc 6th Applied

Natural Language Processing Conference, ANLP-200

- Birant, Ç. C. (2005) Root-Suffix Seperation of Turkish Words, Dokuz Eylul

University, İzmir.

- Alkım, E. (2011) Word Types According to Their Stems, Dokuz Eylul

University, İzmir.

- Toutanova, K & Christopher, D. Manning. (2000) Enriching the Knowledge
  Sources
- Used in a Maximum Entropy Part-of-Speech Tagger. In Proceedings of the Joint

SIGDAT Conference on Empirical Methods in Natural Language Processing and

Very Large Corpora (EMNLP/VLC-2000), pp. 63-70.

- Garside, R. & Leech, G. & . Sampson, G. (eds) (1987) The CLAWS Word-tagging

System. The Computational Analysis of English: A Corpus-based Approach.

London: Longman.

- Altunyurt, L. & Orhan, Z. (June 2006) Submitted to the Department of Computer

Engineering in partial fulfilment of the requirements for the degree of Bachelor

of Science in Computer Engineering, Boğaziçi University

- Rizzolo, N. & Roth D (2010) from

http://cogcomp.cs.illinois.edu/page/software_view/3

- Schmid H. (1993) from
  http://www.ims.unistuttgart.de/projekte/corplex/TreeTagge

- Charniak, E (1997) from http://en.wikipedia.org/wiki/Part-of-speech_tagging

- DeRose, Steven J, (1988) http://en.wikipedia.org/wiki/Part-of-speech_tagging

- Antworth, E. L. (1990) PC-KIMMO: A Two-level Processor for Morphological Analysis. Summer Institute of Linguistics, Dallas, TX.

- Brill, E. (1992) A simple rule-based part-of-speech tagger. In Proceedings of the Third Conference on Applied Computational Linguistics, Trento, Italy.

- Brill, E. (1995) Transformation-based error-driven learning and natural language processing: A case study in part-of-speech tagging. Computational Linguistics, 21(4), 543-566.

- Church, K. W. (1988) A stochastic parts program and noun phrase parser for unrestricted text. In Second Conference on Applied Natural Language Processing,pp.136-143.ACL.

- Cutting, D., & Kupiec, J., & Pedersen, J. O., & Sibun, P. (1992) A practical part-of- speech tagger. In Third Conference on Applied Natural Language Processing, pp.133-140. ACL.

- Dandapat, S., & Sarkar, S., & Basu, A. (2004). A Hybrid Model for Part-of-Speech Tagging and its Application to Bengali. In International Conference on Computational Intelligence, pp. 169-172.

- DeRose, S. J. (1988) Grammatical category disambiguation by statistical optimization. Computational Linguistics, 14, 31-39.

- Jurafsky, D., & Martin, J. H. (2000) Speech and Language Processing: An Introduction to Natural Language Processing, Computational Linguistics, and Speech Recognition. Prentice-Hall, New Jersey.

- Karlsson, F., & Voutilainen, A., & Heikkilä, J., & Anttila, A. (1995) Constraint de Grammar: A Language-Independent System for Parsing Unrestricted Text. Mouton, Gruyter, Berlin.

- Oflazer, K., & Kuruoz, I. (1994). Tagging and morphological disambiguation of Turkish text. In Fourth Conference on Applied Natural Language Processing, pp. 144-149.

- Voutilainen, A. (1995) Morphological disambiguation. In Karlsson, F., Voutilainen, A., Heikkilä, J., and Anttila, A. (Eds.), Constraint Grammar: A Language- Independent System for Parsing Unrestricted Text, pp. 165-284. Mouton de Gruyter,Berlin.

- Dhanalakshmi V, & Anand Kumar M, & Rajendran S, & Soman K P, (2009) POS Tagger and Chunker for Tamil Language Tamil University, Thanjavur, Tamilnadu, India

- Yüzübenli S. (2006) Word Phrases from

  http://anlambilimci.blogspot.com/2006/12/szck-bekleri.html

- İbrahimoğlu İ, (2008) Word Phrases from

  http://konumuzdiledebiyat.blogcu.com/soz-obekleri/3082320

- Güven A, & Bozkurt Ö, & Kalıpsız O. (2006) Gizli Anlambilimsel Dizinleme Yönteminin N- Gram Kelimelerle Geliştirilerek, İleri Düzey Doküman Kümelemesinde Kullanı, ELECO

ABBREVIATIONS

Following acronyms have been used in this thesis:

NLP	Natural Language Processing
NL	Natural
EÖ	Verb Phrase
AÖ	Noun Phrase
İÖ	Preposition Phrase
SÖ	Adjective Phrase
BÖ	Adverb Phrase
E	Verb
A	Noun
B	Adverb
İ	Preposition
S	Adjective

Printed by Books on Demand GmbH, Norderstedt / Germany